Learn and Grow with 64 Sacred Earth Guiding Crystals

This book is about understanding crystalline archetypes and working with eight distinct crystals called the Star Grid. Svetlana's work is inspired by Crystal Alphabet, An Intuitive Guide to rocks and crystals associated with 64 genetic tendencies created by Richard Rudd (Gene Keys, UK). Together these crystals form a global archetypal matrix of the human potential. The choice of crystals is precise and personal.

When we experience fear, anger, or despair, we often lose a perspective of what we are about. Embodying crystalline energy can help you remember who you are and enjoy the true magic of a closer relationship with Earth and each other.

Experience, experiment and explore using your senses. Trust your sensations and allow them to guide you. Every intuitive step you make will create a deeper certainty about your ability to know and perceive non-visible realms.

The purpose of this book is to enhance your life with experiences of magical beauty and power through experimenting with the crystal consciousness. It will initiate your journey into the Field that is beyond your everyday perception. Working with cristalline energy is a pathway into your superconsciousness that will allow you to receive an inner guidance spontaneously and without external help. We are committed to assisting you on your Soul Journey.

With Love,

Svetlana Pritzker, Transformational Counselor and Educator

Alex Drummond, Infiniteus Rocks and Juice Bar, Owner

Your Star Mandala

The Star Mandala is a set of eight influential crystals connected to the eight Gene Keys selected from the sixty-four dynamic forces revealed within your Human Design Mandala.

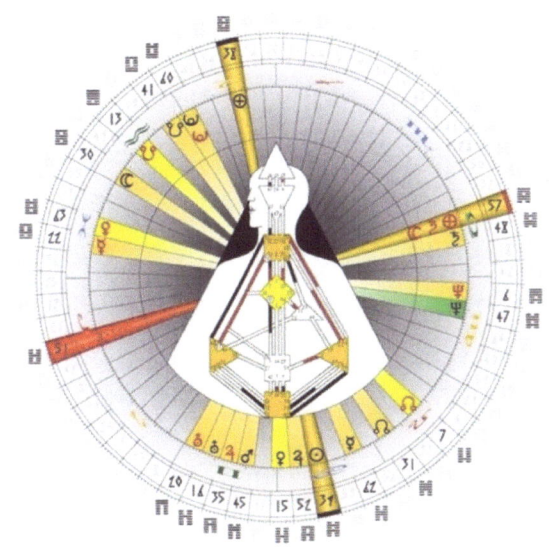

The Mandala on the right is an example how your personal Mandala might look. It is an illustration of the energetic fusions that affected your body at the time of birth. Human Design Coaching is based on the information derived from the BodyGraph in the center of your Mandala. Notice that there are only a few colorful connections between the body inside and the 64 signs forming an outer circle.

Each connection represents a personal trait created by the planetary impact. The meaning of each energetic influence is interpreted during your consultation in connection with the latest scientific discoveries and the wisdom of the ancient healing. The New Human Energetics consultation gives you a practical way to synchronize your individual movement within a greater flow of life by releasing an old conditioning and allowing you to be "in harmony with the Tao". It helps you create the life you want with less effort.

You can find more information at www.energy4action.com or schedule a personal session at Lana@energy4action.com

What is the New Human Energetics

The New Human Energetics is a coaching service based on the Human Design, Gene Keys and Archetypal Flow. It is a new system of self-knowledge that differs fundamentally from anything else that exists in the world today. It is not just built on belief or faith. It is rooted in the Human Design, a logical, empirical system which offers you the opportunity to understand and experiment with your genetic traits and talents, experimenting with your unique strategies for success.

Incorporating quantum physics, biochemistry and genetics with four of the greatest esoteric systems in the world (astrology, the Hindu chakra insight, the Judaic Kabbalah and the Chinese I Ching), this system opens up the realms of self-discovery that are mystical, alchemical and mathematically precise.

About I Ching

Developed more than 5000 years ago, I Ching, the ancient Chinese Book of Changes, describes the evolution of cycles and seasons of life. The binary structure of the Ancient Chinese hexagrams, the Yin and Yang of I Ching, have astonishing similarity to the binary code of our

DNA that is made up of two strands of nucleotides, one strand being an impeccable reflection of the other.

There are four basic permutations of Yin and Yang lines arranged in groups of threes in the ancient I Ching. They are called "trigrams". Each of these trigrams has a partner. Two trigram partners create one of the sixty-four hexagrams of I Ching.

Our genetic code is made up of four 'bases' which are arranged in groups of threes. Each of these chemical groupings relates to an amino acid, forming a set that is known as a "codon". There are 64 of these codons in our genetic code.

Even though each of us is distinctively unique in how we express our inner world, we all share this same basic genetic code. The four bases of our genetic code manifest through our chemistry as four basic types of human beings with a particular strategy for high achievement and fiasco. There are distinct behaviors associated with each of the four types.

Each type (Manifestors, Generators, Projectors and Reflectors) has its area of innate expertise and strategy to be effective in life. Knowing your Human Design type and strategy is like following an operational handbook for life. It helps with the decision-making process, relationship approaches, and financial success tactics. Knowing what and why of your life allows you to be aware and follow your destiny.

Your Type, Strategy and specific genetic strengths revealed in the Design Mandala are based on the date, time, and place of your birth. Your personal data is used to calculate a precise position of your body in the relationship to every planet at the time of your birth. Through the Gene Keys interpretation, this position gives you a biochemical map left in your body by the neutrino stream at the time when you were born.

The personal Human Design Mandala allows you to observe the influences and forces that were magnetized to you at that time and understand the true story of your day to day struggles and victories.

Star Mandala Crystals

The Star Mandala Crystals are a set of eight most powerful stones in your life: Destiny, Lode, Initiator, Wound, Dream, Money, Hoar and Inverse stones. Each of these eight crystals has a specific meaning and effect on your existence.

Dynamic connection with this set will assist you in bringing your body, emotions and mind into an alignment with your Soul Journey. In this book you will learn how to play with each crystal to elevate your consciousness and live in Light, experiencing Love, and speaking the Truth to yourself and others.

The Destiny Stone

Your Destiny Stone is based on your birth information and reflects the exact position of the sun in the Crystal Alphabet when you were born. When it is in your environment, it mirrors your true nature. Further in this book you can see an example of Danburite as a Destiny Stone, but when you receive your eight crystal consultation, the Destiny stone will be different. It will be specifically chosen for you to help you experience Who You Are and what you are here to do in the world.

The Lode Stone

Your Lode Stone is a guardian of your sacred space. It guards your home and increases your understanding of the gentle energies surrounding you and your house. In the "sample crystals" chapter of this book, you will see an example of Celestite as a Lode Stone. With your crystal consultation you will discover the Lode Stone that is not the same because your vibration dictates the choice of the Lode Stone for your house. It is unique to you.

The Initiator Stone

The Initiator Stone acts as a motivator and supporter of your endeavors. It removes obstacles from one's path and helps you integrate change.

The Wound Stone

The Wound Stone echoes your deepest struggles and helps you understand the deepest traumas of your life as an inspiration. It is connected to the most exquisite talents you are destined to bring into the world. It also allows you to transcend the hurt to freely express yourself through creativity, true voice and inspired action.

The Dream Stone

The Dream Crystal is used to enhance your dream life and helps boost your intelligence and memory when you are awake. Further in the book you will learn how to use it for the dream recollection and lucid dreaming.

The Money Stone

Your Money Crystal supports your career choices and helps your be prosperous while doing something you love. It expands your energetic influence so you can effectively manifest what you plan. It also helps you successfully share your talents and be abundant and generous in your life.

The Hoar Stone

The Hoar Crystal connects you to your Spirit and helps you understand the mystical essence within your mundane life. It is a channel through which the flow of the greater Consciousness comes into your field.

The Inverse Stone

The Inverse Crystal brings perspective into your life when you need it most. When you are dealing with a difficult decision or need to move through the chaos, this crystal will help you relax and find the best

pathway through the challenges and obstacles. It is a grounding stone at the time of crisis.

The crystalline energy guides your Super Consciousness with the flow of light that they radiate. Each of the eight stones chosen from your Mandala emits power that is recognized by your DNA. This energy reminds you to follow the flow of life, to slow down and pay attention.

Each stone opens a portal into the universe of experiences. We recommend exploring each of your crystals alone before setting them up as a grid. Listening to the inner voice and sensations you experience while working with different crystals will help you open your consciousness to the multidimensional perception and make decisions that are rooted in certainty, vision and an understanding of the bigger picture of your life. The purpose of this work is to teach you feel where and when the flow of your life is ready to move forward and be able to take a giant step toward your goal when you are truly ready.

Lights and Colors

Color is a form of observable light. Every primary color that is reflected in the rainbow transmits a unique healing energy. It is important to feel, see and know the colors that match your needs and use their healing power when you are facing a difficult situation.

Color therapy, also called chromo therapy, is a form of the vibrational treatment that integrates the chi energies within living organisms. The colors of gemstones and crystals are the vibrational remedies that can shift misalignments into more harmonious states we associate with wellbeing.

The impact of each singular crystal could be further enhanced by using a variety of lights. This chapter will teach you to use crystals to apply color therapy principles in your everyday life. Play with the different crystals and colors as you learn to permeate light in the

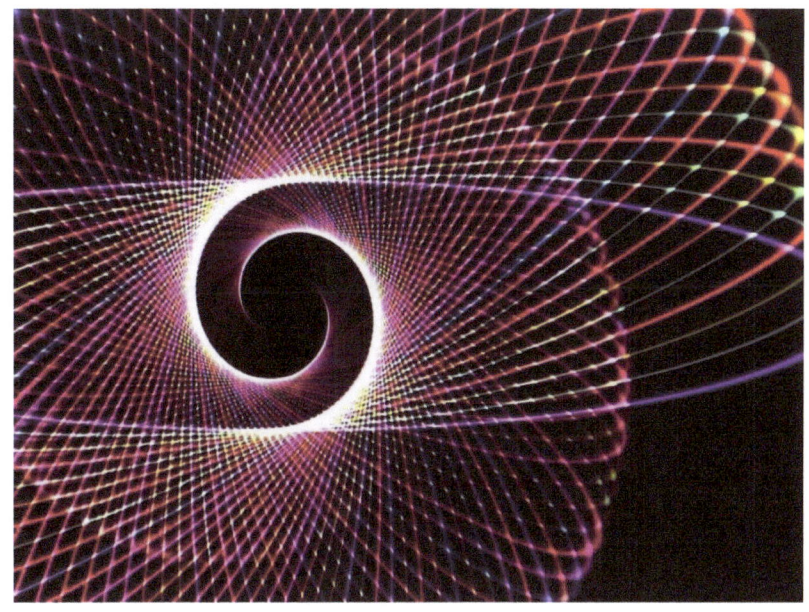

areas where your life needs healing. We suggest using colors from both lasers and crystals to enhance your intentions and balance your physical, emotional, spiritual, and mental health.

Use each of the Eight Star Crystals in combination with the color awareness to help invigorate different areas of your life that are lacking vibrancy. For each of your objectives, choose the color to work with intuitively or follow the color description below. Choose an intention and direct a laser beam to any facet or point of the crystal to experience the unity with light.

White is an all-encompassing color.

It stimulates healing at all levels, guiding pain, stress, and negativity out from your energy field.

Red is a color of survival.

Red stirs up the entire body field, stimulates your immune system and boosts the energy levels. It assists in raising frequencies of vitality and passion. The color Red is associated with healing sexual dysfunctions and positively influencing reproduction and fertility.

Orange is a color of personal power.

Orange is helpful for soothing aches in joints and muscles, normalizing weak pulse rate, resolving gall bladder and kidney problems, allergies and fatigue.

Yellow is a color of self-respect.

Yellow relaxes the nervous system, calms digestive issues and helps release skin problems.

The color yellow promotes a healthy metabolism; reduces anxiety and stress related disorders. It balances emotions and strengthens the level of toleration if you are over-sensitive.

Green is a color of open-heartedness.

Green helps to fight infections and viruses. It supports the heart, lungs, and respiratory system. Working with green helps reduce panic attacks, addictions, and longing. The green color delivers a wave of protective masculine love.

The blue color supports your inner authority and manifestation.

Blue is naturally soothing and refreshing. Use blue when you need to lower blood pressure, relieve headaches, earache, and sore throat. It also delivers an empowering energy to your voice and manifestations.

The purple color is connected to the higher mind/intuitive knowing.

Purple is useful for healing the wounded spirit, forgiving and letting go of the past and eliminating neuroses and obsessions. Purple is very versatile and naturally relaxing as it unlocks your mind to the wisdom of higher perspectives.

The pink/fuchsia color opens a channel into the higher realm and its guidance.

Fuchsia brings a sense of oneness, helps release the mental oppression and limiting believes that generate psychosomatic disorders. This color also carries an energetic wave of unconditional feminine love.

The brown color is associated with feeling safe and secure.

The spectrum of the natural brown radiates neutrality and helps you let

go of worries. Permeating brown through your body allows you experience a sense of certainty and inner strength.

For example, play with a smoky quartz crystal and a white laser to create deep healing. Saturate the area that needs to be repaired with color and light. Visualize the color and light infusing this area with healing vibrations.

Be patient and witness how you influenced your body wellbeing with the natural brown color of the smoky quartz enhanced with the full spectrum of white light.

1. When you feel unsafe or uncomfortable, imagine sending any shade of brown through your body. You can start from your feet or imagine pouring this color from the top of your head down your spine.
2. Notice the state of relaxation and ease that comes with the brown color.

Sending this color through your body helps get rid of problems with the skeleton and lower extremities and improves the functionality of the large intestine.

Each session, however short, connects you with the mineral kingdom and its extensive library of the Earth history. Working with each color emitted by the eight crystals of your Star Mandala awakes your latent therapeutic potential. Each healing session initiates a personal resonance with the pure crystalline light that is within your reach.

Using lasers for Light and Color healing is well researched and documented. The bright light affects the brain chemicals that are responsible for the positive outlook on life, prevention of the mood swings and a restful sleep. Using white or colored lasers with your crystals may help you alleviate blues produced by the luck of the full spectrum light during the fall and winter seasons. It may reduce the symptoms of sleep disorders or any other dis-ease you experience.

Crystalline Grids

You can start by acquiring one stone at a time or buy a whole set at once.

When you buy a whole set, we will provide you with a personalized booklet of metaphysical meaning, healing properties and instructions for working with each of your individual crystal or stone.

Even though each crystal is a powerhouse, the impact of the crystal grid is even stronger. The grid amplifies intentions placed within the geometric pattern of its structure and directs the energy toward your spiritual goal as a transformative experience. Each crystal is cleansed, re-charged or re-programmed when placed within the energetic field of the grid.

The Life Booster Grid

In addition to the eight initial crystals of the Star Grid, you have other planetary and I Ching activations within your Human Design Mandala. Each of them resonates with a specific stone that might not be included in your Star Mandala. If you are mesmerized by the beauty and mystery of the crystals, you might enjoy working with the Life Booster Grid – the full set of all crystals and stones connected to energies in your Human Design.

The Life Booster grid might consist of 15 – 25 crystals that uplift the most important aspects of your life and gives you endless inspiration for self-discovery, astral travel, and deep inner expansion. Initiated by the different crystals that reflect your light and power, you would be able to let go of the imprints that undermine your integrity and start making decisions based on your real values and priorities.

Guidelines for Creating a Crystal Grid

These instructions will help you to set up various crystal grids and use them to positively influence different areas of your life. Remember, there are no strict rules or regulations when it comes to playing in the field of super consciousness. The grid is a powerful container of your intention and inspiration. Allow your imagination to guide you in this spiritual journey.

1. Choose the purpose of your new grid. Express your intent in a direct and precise sentence.

2. Find a location where your grid will not be disturbed.

2. Create a sacred space for your grid. Cleanse this space using intention, burning sage, or sound (For example, music or clapping your hands).

3. Think about how you would like to position yourself. You can sit inside a larger shape or project your energy into a smaller structure set in front of you.

4. Form a crystal layout using circular or an octagonal pattern or follow any other geometry that feels right at the moment.

5. Write your intention on a piece of paper or on the back of an image that resonates with your goal. Place your intentional note inside the grid.

6. Relax from head to toes. Breathe from your center into the center of your grid. Focus on seeing your intention as already realized.

7. Ask: How would it feel if this intention was already fulfilled? Choose the words that describe your experience. What are the words, emotions, and sensations that you'd like to amplify and support yourself with? (See the list of empowering words at the end of this booklet. It will help you choose different vibrational qualities for your practice.)

8. Stay in this vibration and cultivate it within for a few minutes. You need some time to embody this state.

9. Feel the joy and gratitude of having what you want. Allow these vibrations to emanate, warming up your heart and bringing a smile to your face.

10. When you are done using the grid, you can clean the energy by clapping around your crystals, bathing your crystals in the sunshine or washing them with natural water (For example, rain or lake water).

Intentions and Manifestations

Use one crystal at a time to get to know their energy. Hold each crystal in your hands. Notice any changes in temperature or vibration of your hands or any other part of your body.

1. Create an anchor for your intention. Holding your crystal, create an affirmation/intention you want to program into your crystal.

2. Repeat this affirmation or intention three times. It will be embodied by the crystal you

want to program. Seeing or touching this crystal each time will evoke your intent and call you into action.

3. Give each stone a particular intentional quality. It will help you be more efficient in setting up your goals and following through with them. Program each crystal for one task to avoid energy diffusion.

4. Entrain with the high vibrations of the crystal realm. Focus on one Star Mandala stone and one area of your life for at least one week (see the list of crystals and their purpose in the "Star Mandala Meaning" chapter).

4. Be mindful of the physical sensations through which your body communicates with you. Learn what feels right and what creates a shrinking pattern in your body and life. Pay attention to subtle senses.

5. Ask your crystals to share their wisdom. Follow through with the insights and healing messages you receive from each of them. Make

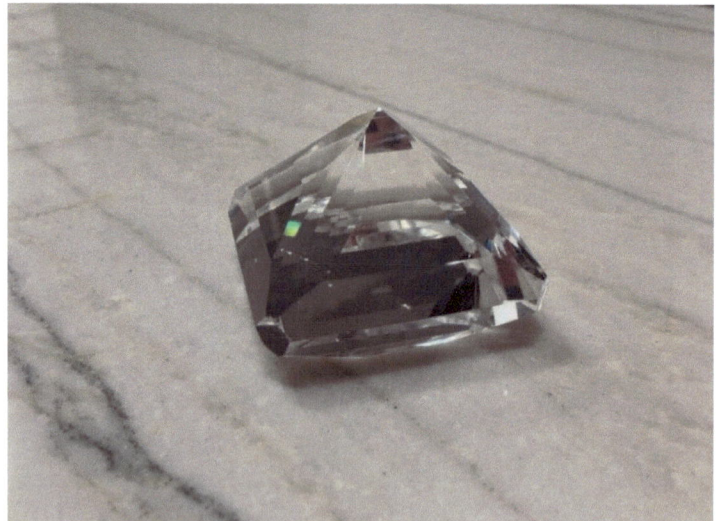

changes directed by these communications.

6. Continue engaging with your stones on a regular basis. Focus on their beauty and vibratory influence on you. This practice helps detach from fearful thoughts, body "problems" based on mental/emotional limitations

and let go of the abusive relationships. In time, you will begin naturally re-direct your thoughts away from difficulties and toward opportunities that are hidden in each "problem".

7. Remember that your emotional state influences the energy of others in your environment. Impact others with the energy of well-being and find a personal sense of significance and connection through this positive contribution.

8. Use these affirmations to connect to the never-ending stream of life energy expressed as Earth gems.

"I am a big spirit. I am an important part of creation. I matter".

9. Ask each of your crystals about what you are destined to do at this moment of your life. Record these answers. They will assist in bringing your body, emotions and mind into an alignment with your Soul Journey. Each of such experiences opens the next level of connection and oneness with your purpose on the planet Earth.

The Master Grid

Crystal grids are extremely influential, especially when you are placing your stones in a geometric pattern that directs their energy toward your spiritual goal and healing intention placed inside.

Star Crystals as the Master Grid

Your Star Grid (the eight initial stones) can be used as a "Master Grid", a network that amplifies and grounds the life force intended for each of your manifestations. If you wish to re-charge your stones, crystals or spiritual tools, place them inside the Star Grid and set an intention to positively influence that which is inside the grid.

Astral Travel with the Master Grid

1. Set the Star Grid: relax and place each of your eight stones in a place that feels right. You can also use octagonal shapes of the Sacred Geometry.

2. Set an intention for this grid to focus and amplify your multidimensional experience.

3. Set an intention for this Astral Travel. Repeat it three times as a statement, not as a question. Make sure it is clear, concise and purposeful.

For example:

I travel to explore a past lifetime that is affecting my business life now.

I go to discover a lifetime that is significant to my physical well-being and health right now.

I travel to a period that influenced my relationship with...

You can also set an intention to explore your lives in ancient civilizations such as Lemuria and Atlantis, the times when you worked with magic or the lives when you turned away from your mystical core.

1. Intent to stay safe and trust the guidance through sensations and images.

2. Now think of some place that feels comfortable and secure. "Stay" there and cultivate the feeling of safety. When you feel safe and comfortable, set an intention to experience the same feeling while having a new Astral Travel.

3. Imagine yourself standing at the top of a staircase, looking down.

4. Intend to stay connected to your body and feelings throughout your journey. Anything you might experience from the fear and anxiety to the excitement and curiosity is important and valid information. Allow yourself to feel all your sensations as waves of energy and information without labeling them in any way.

5. Begin your descent by stepping down one step at a time. You can start with any foot, left or right. Bring the other foot down to join your first foot. Alternate your feet as you are stepping down and counting from 10 all the way to 1.

6. At the bottom of the staircase, "see" or imagine a long corridor with a door at the end. As you walk the hallway, repeat your intention for this experience three times.

7. Now you stand at the door. Say the following: "I am now going to step into a special place and time in a circle of life." Say it again while touching the door knob, turning the knob and then opening the door.

8. Keep walking, step in and over the threshold. Wait and let the energies to adjust. Allow a new experience to come to you. Save it in your Journal.

The Dream Grid

The Dream Grid could be built with the same Dream Stones (based on your Human Design BodyGraph) or with a set of your Star Crystals and one Dream Stone positioned in a center of the grid.

It is best to work with each crystal alone at first to get to know its frequency. Then you can start experimenting with pairs, trios and other combinations. Each new crystal in combination with the dream Stone will help intensify your premonitions as well as add a new dimension to your dreams and visions.

Eventually, you will train yourself to recognize the energy emitted by each crystal. This is the time to use the whole Star Grid or more than a couple of stones to form bigger, more powerful grids. Each specific circle interacts uniquely with the Dream Stone inside and affects your dream life in a different way. With practice, you will become very accurate in choosing the crystals to form a magic circle for each intention.

Place an intention (written on a piece of paper) under the Dream Stone. This will help you establish a conscious connection with your dream world and recall dreams easier.

Make sure to connect with your grid by touching the crystals and entraining with their vibration before falling asleep.

With its crystalline vibrations, the Dream Grid deepens your understanding of messages delivered during your sleep and opens the portals into angelic realms.

Recalling Your Dreams with the Dream Grid

1. Set your crystals or clusters under the bed or somewhere in your bedroom. Be creative or use sacred geometry patterns to form the grid.

2. Think of an intention before you go to sleep. Decide where you would like to travel and who do you who to connect with. Are there any Masters or Universes you are interested in visiting?

3. Fill up a glass of water before going to bed. Make an intention to anchor your dreams and drink ½ of it before going to sleep.

4. With an intention to fully recall your dream upon awakening, state it

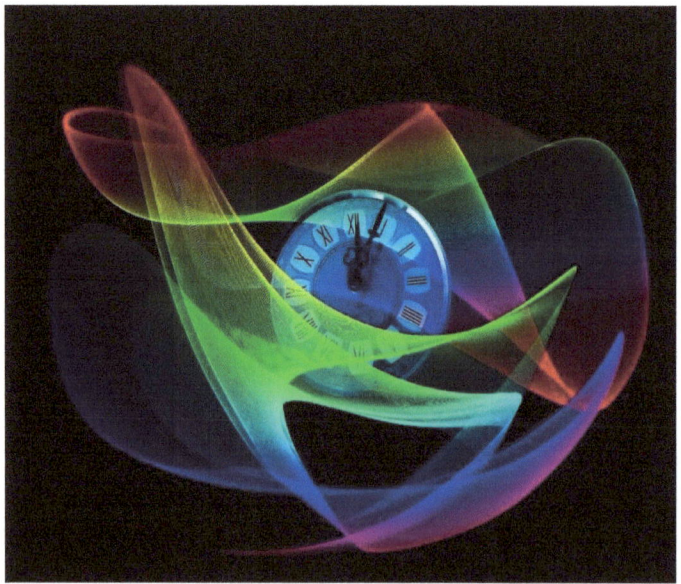

out loud: "When I drink the other half, I will remember my dream."

5. After you wake up, drink the other half to remember your astral travel and journal insights you have gained.

6. If you have unresolved matter, ask your Dream Crystal to show you the way to resolve it or a person who might be

helpful in finding a solution to the problem.

7. Keep a notebook on your nightstand for recording thoughts and images right as you wake up.

Crystals will enhance your dream time learning process, amplify intentions and bring purity to your dreams. They also add a spiritual atmosphere to your bedroom environment.

Past Lives - Ancient Libraries

Exploring multidimensional realities perceived as Past and Future Lives or Parallel Universes can help you understand and eradicate repetitive issues and conditioned behaviors that create problems in the present time. Working with past lifetimes and other dimensions or realities enhances your personal growth, generates clarity of perception and builds trust in the power of your inner authority.

In this chapter, you will learn to release unnecessary stress and re-connect with powerful skills and knowledge from the past using each journey as your power laboratory.

Visiting Influential Life Times

1. Hold your dream stone. Intend to visit a life time where you had an influential position or acquired a powerful skill.

2. Intend to internally integrate these skills and power into your current life.

3. Intend to come back to current life time supported, relaxed and ready for action within not more than 30 minutes.

4. Relax your body and count backward from ten to one.

5. With "one" arrive at a place and time you want to explore. Notice colors and sensations associated with this place and time.

6. Bring all the sensations and visions into your focus. Be a "visitor" and witness all that you see, feel or know about it. Be patient with yourself. Allow knowing, sensations or images to appear.

7. When conscious, bring in the colors of the place you are visiting or take a virtual souvenir such as tool you used or book you found to remember this place and time. Place the souvenir in your virtual pocket. When you are in the deep unconscious state throughout the journey, trust this will be done by intent.

8. Come to the present time whenever you are ready. Ask your consciousness to recall and integrate all of the experiences.

9. Ask yourself: "How would I act (or make a decision) if I would have this information, skills, and power in my life right now?"

If you discover that there was a time when you were disempowered or unappreciated, you can change this experience by re-visiting this lifetime in a meditative state.

1. Imagine you are there again.
2. Connect to this place by breathing in all the colors that remind you of it. Observe anything that comes to your mind's eye.
3. In your mind, re-picture an experience when you lost your authority in a way that makes you feel powerful again.
4. Now breathe in all the colors from that new experience and embody your power and inner strength.
5. Come back to the present time. Imagine yourself making decisions and acting from this power and authority in a difficult situation you are facing now. Stay in the field of power you've created. Remember that you

always have the power and an authority to change hurtful memories and re-set any negative influences to free your mind and feel better.

Star Crystals Consultation

Below is a short non-personalized version of the information you will receive during your Star Mandala Consultation. The personal experience includes your BodyGraph with the Chakra Assessment helping you understand the energetic influences within your vital centers. Per your request, it might have an emphasis on any single stone from your Star

Grid or the download about each of the eight Star Crystals.

The sample we have included in this book contains information about two randomly chosen stones, but during your Star Mandala consultation, you will receive information about and instructions for working with your particular stones. Your Life Purpose, relationship, and personal success strategies will also be revealed.

Danburite as Your Destiny Stone

Danburite is a great stone that initiates an action when you are facing a pivotal point in your life. It is a stone that brings awareness to imbalances in your life and opens your mind to new possibilities and intuitive solutions.

Danburite helps you see where injustice is present in your life and assist you in finding a path to equilibrium and harmony. At its highest frequency, it connects you to the harmony of the Celestial Spheres.

A very powerful and a highly spiritual crystal, Danburite emanates a sweet and pure vibration that is incredibly uplifting to the spirit. It helps you shift from being irresponsible or over reactive to more harmonious thoughts and actions.

Danburite directs your attention to finding more equilibrium within your life. It gently yet powerfully opens the Crown Chakra and attunes it to the Heart chakra. The energetic connecting between these two centers shifts your intellectual viewpoint into a higher consciousness that is based on a heart-centered perspective.

Danburite may be colorless, pale pink or golden yellow. Sometimes you can see fascinating prismatic configurations or a Buddha-like formation inside. This stone is believed to promote ascension and embodiment of self-love.

Danburite increases the spiritual light of anyone who uses it. In any color, it is an amazing tool for spiritual growth and deep connection to the higher consciousness.

Use these affirmations to program your crystal.

I find harmony in everything.

I look for harmony even at the time of chaos.

Evoke Your Destiny with Danburite

Danburite has highly beneficial metaphysical properties. During the meditation, Pink Danburite takes you to a state of consciousness within which you connect with your spirit guides and access their teachings.

Danburite brings the harmony from the angelic realm down into the human heart. The pink variety is especially beneficial for the Heart Chakra as it can help you experience unconditional feminine love.

At times of overwhelm accompanied by uncontrolled feelings triggered by past events or current misunderstanding, Danburite helps bring a deep sense of patience and peace. It can assist with emotional healing and release of anxiety. You can also use the yellow Danburite for lucid dreaming.

With consistent practice, you will become more aware of what is happening while you are asleep and will begin to observe your states and what you might feel almost as if you were awake.

Golden yellow Danburite connects you to the sweetness of etheric music. It helps you experience deeper self-respect and trust in your higher self. This variety attunes you to the wisdom of your Soul so you can move forward in a new direction with ease and confidence.

Danburite has both strong cleansing and detoxifying effects. It works with the energy of the liver, removing unwanted toxins, helping restore the musculature and clear allergic over-reactions.

Celestite as the Lode Stone

Cool and shiny, Celestite contains the explosive energy of the final blast of the superstar. It is also called Supernova. Supernova is an old star that continuously grows and eventually expands outwardly with an

explosion. This process symbolizes transmutation of the energy through detachment and rebirth into the myriads of new elements of creation.

Celestite helps sustain the efforts. It brings the energy of everlasting expansion, creativity, and explosive radiance. Its presence in your home boosts your creative genius and inspires to manifest your dreams. Celestite is a portal into the light consciousness.

The name Celestite comes from a Latin word that means "heaven." Its energy supports your quest for personal authority that is based on self-respect and channeled in a form of the celestial guidance.

The archetypal energies within this crystal are the supernova, endurance, passion and willingness to go an extra mile to accomplish your goals.

Danburite helps release stress and tension. It directs your energy into the creative flow and shifts your state from being dreamy or hyperactive into a vibration of sustained interest leading to the manifestation of your dreams into a material form.

Celestite crystals mined in Ohio are the most potent ones. They are usually blue or grayish blue, but there are also clear, white, green, yellowish, orange or reddish brown specimens.

Playing with the Celestite's Energy

Celestite's energy is gentle, radiant and elevating.

Its crystals are pointing in all directions, creating a feeling of expansion, lightness and inspiration. Set intent to understand and unlock limiting patterns hidden within your home.

Spend a few minutes moving around and sensing subtle energies amplified by your crystal. This practice will increase your awareness of the unseen realms.

Tender, yet robust, Celestite is helpful in the opening of the Third Eye. It directs your focus to higher dimensions, enhances your divine intuition, strengthens psychic abilities and improves mental capacity for learning and living on purpose.

1. Focus your attention on the

Celestite cluster and make a few continues conscious breaths by inhaling for five counts and exhaling for six without stopping. This practice helps you let go of anxiety and obsessive behaviors that are produced by the lack of purpose and limited self-expression.

2. With its blue radiation, Celestite supports Throat chakra and helps alleviate any stage fright, fear of public speaking and dread of crowds. Holding your crystals, make an intention to let go of the fears and express yourself fully even in a difficult situation. Then imagine yourself being strong and communicative in one of such circumstances and let the Celestite energy help you feel calmer and more confident. Cultivate these feelings for a few minutes.

3. Celestite harmonizes and balances one's energetic field. It helps shy adults and children stand up for themselves and try new experiences. Danburite also facilitates deep states during meditation and assist in speaking your truth and sharing your visions with perfect clarity. It promotes peaceful, wholesome approach to life and helps integrate higher perspectives into your daily living.

Healing Properties of Celestite

Celestine is working primarily with the Throat Chakra, but it also influences the function of Crown, Third Eye, and Solar Star Chakras.

At a physical level, it works with joint alignments and reduces the chronic pain. It increases hearing, eliminates headaches, assists with sleeping issues (including sleep apnea), and harmonizes misalignments connected to the throat chakra such as thyroid, etc.

Emotional ailments include overcoming depression, finding forgiveness, learning to forgive, to trust and to find peaceful solutions.

Recommended Intentions

Hold your Celestite crystal or position it where you can see it. Ask for its protection and help in becoming more clairaudient. Make an intention to receive deeper mental clarity and ask for energetic support of your true voice. It will help you improve your communication patterns.

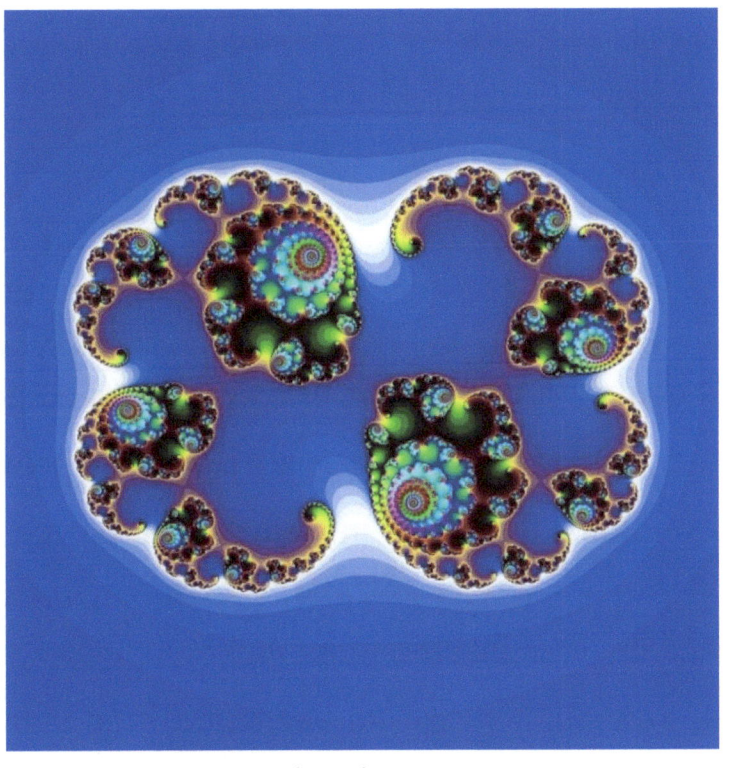

If you are looking for celestial foresight and understanding of your Destiny, ask Celestite to help you find your true calling and direct your efforts to live in the light.

Suggestions for Affirmations

1. I am a channel of light.
2. Timeless light is always flowing through me.
3. I receive clear communication from divine realms.

Guarding Your Space

The purpose of Celestite as the Lode Stone is to shield your home and harmonize the energy of your sacred space. It initiates a clear understanding of the energy behind your usual perception so you can organize your space in a more creative and effective way.

1. Start by visiting each area of your home.

2. Holding Celestite in your hands, notice where your attention is guided.

3. You might see some things that need to be removed or moved around. Act on your intuition and make your space feel right for you.

4. You might also feel like something is missing. Ask: "What do I need to change right here?" Act on the guidance you receive.

5. Spend a few minutes "consulting" the Lode Stone. Ask any question that comes to your mind. For example: "What is your message about my space?"

6. "What would make this area more inspiring, more elevated for me, my work, my family?" Write down the messages you receive. They might deliver exactly the guidance you were seeking.

The Lode Stone could be buried beneath the foundation, but it is also beneficial to place Celestite at the center of your home. It will strongly affect the geomagnetic currents surrounding your house and increase your sensitivity to all energies around or within your house.

Restore and Renew

To clean and renew the energy in your room, place one of your Lode crystals in a window. The sunlight or natural light will permeate through this crystal and emanate out re-programmed rays. It might also add sparkling light prisms and rid your room of the negative energies.

These emissions usually form an energetic lattice of light that creates more harmony and balance within your space and sends positive energy throughout.

1. If you have a few crystals, or a full Star Mandala set, place these gems in a geometrical shape where they can catch the sunlight (or set your grid outside on a sunny day). Place Celestite in the center.

2. Position yourself in the center of the grid holding Celestite or imagine yourself inside if you have built a smaller grid. You can use simple shapes like triangle, circle, square.

3. Look at the light radiating from the crystals and imagine different colors entering your body.

4. Pay attention to the sensations each color produces. Notice how being inside this grid affects you?

5. Remember to breathe as you are experimenting with your crystals. This practice will attune you to your home and create a harmonious feeling of wellbeing.

Reprogram Yourself

When you feel awkward or your emotions are triggered by some memory from the past, you can reprogram your responses by using the full Star Grid or any single crystal.

1. Intuitively chose a crystal or a pair of gems from your Star Grid that draws your attention at the

moment. Hold them in your hands and allow their beauty and power to re-focus your attention inwardly.

2. Feel the new energy entering your being and be grateful for a gift of life at this moment, no matter how difficult it may be.

Being alive means you have survived up to this point, and you have the power to make decisions that help you survive in the future. It means you can create the change you desire.

Be the Word

Find a word that expresses what you need or value you live by. Choose the words that give you the support you need at the moment.

1. Repeat this word three times and feel its sound resonating within your body and into your crystals. Notice the inner response.

2. Holding your crystals, inhale for five counts and exhale for six counts. Imagine that you "inhale" the word you have chosen and "exhale" the word "stress".

3. Repeat this exercise 3 – 5 times and notice how you feel. Most

people report feeling at peace and in balance after bringing in the words matching their innermost values and desires.

Below is the list of words you can choose from or think of any other word you want. They represent our collective ideals expressed as the Gifts of the Full Spectrum of Consciousness (Richard Rudd, Gene Keys, UK).

These words will remind you that you are the Being of Light having a spiritual experience called Human Life and will help you attune to your true nature.

Freshness, Orientation, Innovation, Understanding, Patience, Diplomacy, Guidance, Style, Determination, Naturalness, Idealism, Discrimination, Discernment, Competence, Magnetism, Versatility, Far-sightedness Integrity, Sensitivity, Self-Assurance, Authority, Graciousness, Simplicity, Invention, Acceptance, Artfulness, Altruism, Totality, Commitment, Lightness, Leadership, Conservation, Mindfulness, Strength, Adventure, Humanity, Equality, Perseverance, Dynamism, Resolve, Anticipation, Detachment, Insight, Teamwork, Synthesis, Delight, Resourcefulness, Initiative, Expansion.

ABOUT THE AUTHOR

Svetlana Pritzker is the founder of New Human Energetics, a system that helps people discover their true calling, overcome challenges and live on purpose. With extensive knowledge and experience in education and energy work, she is highly passionate about helping you find the magical experiences in your life and raise inspired and empowered children.

Svetlana is an author of several books about co-creating relationships of love and trust and co-parenting motivated and capable children. She generously shares her wisdom and expertize on the YouTube channel at www.youtube.com/Lanapritzker

To learn about her work and to book a personal or a group session or an event, visit www.energy4action.com or email Lana@energy4action.com

Special thanks to the contributors of https://pixabay.com for permission to use their royalty free photos as a base for crafting some of the illustrations for this book.

Copyright © 2016 Svetlana Pritzker